DEB
HAALAND

DEB HAALAND

First Native American Cabinet Secretary

JILL DOERFLER

MATTHEW J. MARTINEZ

LERNER PUBLICATIONS ◆ MINNEAPOLIS

DEDICATED TO THE WATER PROTECTORS AND STEWARDS OF THE LAND

Lerner Publications Company
An imprint of Lerner Publishing Group, Inc.
241 First Avenue North
Minneapolis, MN 55401 USA

For reading levels and more information, look up this title at www.lernerbooks.com.

Image credits: U.S. Department of the Interior, pp. 2, 6; AP Photo/Alex Brandon, p. 8; Official White House Photo by Cameron Smith/flickr, p. 10; Shannon R Stevens/Shutterstock.com, p. 12; Volker Schmidt/flickr (CC0 1.0), p. 13; Natalia Bratslavsky/Shutterstock.com, p. 14; Raisa Nastukova/iStock/Getty Images, p. 17; LauriPatterson/iStock/Getty Images, p. 18; Roberto E. Rosales/Albuquerque Journal/ZUMA Press Inc/Alamy Stock Photo, p. 21; Terray Sylvester/VWPics via AP Images, p. 22; Deb Haaland/Wikimedia Commons (public domain), p. 24; Leila Navidi/Star Tribune via AP, p. 25; Graeme Jennings/Pool via AP, p. 28; Jeffhollett/Wikimedia Commons (CC BY-SA 4.0), p. 29; Marc Toso/AncientSkys Photography/Wikimedia Commons (CC BY-SA 4.0), p. 30; Abaca Press/Alamy Stock Photo, p. 33; AP Photo/Matt Rourke, p. 36; AP Photo/Jose Luis Magana, p. 37; AP Photo/J. Scott Applewhite, p. 39. Cover: NPS/Jacob W. Frank/flickr.

Main body text set in Rotis Serif Std 55 Regular. Typeface provided by Adobe Systems.

Designer: Lauren Cooper

Library of Congress Cataloging-in-Publication Data

Names: Martinez, Matthew J., author. | Doerfler, Jill, author.
Title: Deb Haaland : first Native American cabinet secretary / Matthew J. Martinez, Jill Doerfler.
Description: Minneapolis, MN : Lerner Publications, [2023] | Series: Gateway biographies | Includes
  bibliographical references and index. | Audience: Ages 9–14 | Audience: Grades 4–6 | Summary: "In
  2021, Deb Haaland made history as the first Indigenous cabinet secretary. Serving as secretary of the
  interior, Haaland has championed climate and the rights of Native peoples. Discover Haaland's early
  life, her political career, and more"— Provided by publisher.
Identifiers: LCCN 2021060714 (print) | LCCN 2021060715 (ebook) | ISBN 9781728458458 (library
  binding) | ISBN 9781728463186 (paperback) | ISBN 9781728461298 (ebook)
Subjects: LCSH: Cabinet officers—United States—Biography—Juvenile literature. | United States.
  Department of the Interior—Officials and employees—Juvenile literature. | Women cabinet officers—
  United States—Biography—Juvenile literature. | Pueblo Indians—Biography—Juvenile literature. |
  Indian legislators—United States—Biography—Juvenile literature. | Women legislators—United States—
  Biography—Juvenile literature. | Legislators—New Mexico—Biography—Juvenile literature. | Indians of
  North America—United States—Social conditions—Juvenile literature.
Classification: LCC E901.1.H33 M37 2022 (print) | LCC E901.1.H33 (ebook) | DDC 328.73/092 [B]—
  dc23/eng/20220112

LC record available at https://lccn.loc.gov/2021060714
LC ebook record available at https://lccn.loc.gov/2021060715

Manufactured in the United States of America
1-50874-50211-4/5/2022

TABLE OF CONTENTS

Deb Haaland smiles in her official photo as secretary of the interior.

On March 18, 2021, Deb Haaland walked into the Eisenhower Executive Office Building in Washington, DC, wearing a colorful ribbon skirt and tall, white Laguna Pueblo moccasins. She took a deep breath as she raised her right hand. Vice President Kamala Harris swore her in as the fifty-fourth US secretary of the interior. Haaland's family stood next to her in support. They cheered when the oath was complete. That day, Haaland became the first Native American to lead a cabinet agency in the United States. It was a historic and special day for her and her family as well as for Native Americans across the US.

Harris (*right*) swears Haaland (*left*) in as secretary of the interior.

Many people noticed Haaland's outfit. Some Americans had never seen a Native American ribbon skirt before. They wanted to know more about it.

Haaland had known that what she would wear to the ceremony was important. She liked to pick outfits with special meanings and connections to her identity. And she thought a ribbon skirt might be just the thing.

Ribbon skirts are long, hand-sewn skirts that feature rows of ribbon. Some have special designs that tell a story. For generations, Native Americans have made these skirts and worn them for ceremonies. In recent years, more Native American women have worn ribbon skirts at public political events like the Dakota Access Pipeline protests.

There are many different teachings about ribbon skirts. Generally these skirts symbolize Native American women's power and honor female ancestors. Ribbon skirts unite Native American women and serve as a reminder that all choices and actions will impact future generations.

Haaland picked a skirt designed and made by Agnes Woodward. Woodward is Plains Cree from the Kawacatoose First Nation in Saskatchewan, Canada. The royal blue skirt was decorated with rainbow ribbons, which represent all people. The cornstalk design represents Haaland's Pueblo heritage. Haaland asked that two butterflies be added to give the skirt an uplifting message.

Woodward was honored to make the skirt. She said that the ribbon skirt "reminds us of the matriarchal power we carry as Indigenous women. [Ribbon skirts] carry stories of survival, resilience, adaptation, and sacredness. As survivors of genocide we wear our ribbon skirts to stay grounded in our teachings, to stay connected to the earth and our ancestors."

The symbolism of the ribbon skirt reflected Haaland's goals as she started her new job. In one of her first actions as secretary, she announced that she would create a unit focused on pursuing justice for murdered and missing Indigenous women.

Haaland (*right*) wears a ribbon skirt to her swearing-in ceremony. Her skirt features a cornstalk and butterflies.

Another of Haaland's top priorities was to address climate change so that lands and resources won't be damaged beyond repair. She promised to deal with environmental issues that affect communities, including health problems related to pollution. Haaland said, "Every single decision that we make today is going to impact generations to come."

EARLY YEARS

Guwaadzi hauba—greetings. This simple act of introduction in the Keres language speaks of a deep connection to place and people. Keres is one of many Indigenous languages spoken in New Mexico. Deb Haaland is an enrolled citizen of a Keres-speaking nation known as Laguna Pueblo, located about 45 miles (72 km) west of Albuquerque, New Mexico. Six villages make up Laguna Pueblo.

Sovereign Nations

Sovereignty is the authority to govern and make laws. Native American nations existed long before the United States. The US Constitution and federal laws still recognize their sovereignty. This means Native Americans have a unique relationship with the US government. Native Americans belong to three polities, or distinct political entities. They are US citizens, members of the state where they live, and citizens of their tribal nation. There are currently 574 Native American nations within the US, each with its own distinct governing bodies, language, and customs.

Haaland is a member of the Laguna Pueblo. The nation's traditional name is K'awaika. Its reservation features mesas.

Indigenous peoples have lived and thrived in the Southwest since time immemorial. Many of them were farmers and built their homes in villages. When Spanish people arrived in the 1500s, they called the Indigenous people who lived there "Pueblo" because it means "townspeople" in Spanish. The name Pueblo is still used, but Pueblos have always referred to themselves by their original names. For instance, Tuah-tah (Taos Pueblo) is a Tiwa word that means Place of the Red Willows. And Nanbé Owingeh (Nambé Pueblo) in Tewa translates to Place of the Rounded Earth. Pueblo names, like the names of most Native American communities, describe the land and are important to honoring a place.

Laguna is a Spanish word for lake. So the name Laguna Pueblo is a reference to a nearby lake. The nation's traditional Keres name is K'awaika. In modern times, there are about twenty Pueblo nations. They include members living in their home communities as well as those who live and work throughout New Mexico and beyond.

Debra Anne Haaland was born in 1960 in Winslow, Arizona, to a K'awaika mother and a Norwegian American father. She grew up in a military family. Her mother, Mary Toya, served in the navy and worked at the Bureau of Indian Education for twenty-five years. Deb's father, John David "Dutch" Haaland, spent thirty years in the United States Marine Corps. He received the Silver Star for his service in Vietnam.

Winslow's historic downtown

Haaland often returned to the K'awaika reservation to spend time with her grandparents, Tony Toya and Helen Steele.

As a military family, the Haalands moved frequently. Deb learned to adapt to new places and people. Practicing the K'awaika values of respect and compassion helped her make friends wherever she went.

Mary Toya wanted Deb to have strong K'awaika connections even though the family moved a lot. She made sure that Deb spent a lot of time with her grandparents, Helen Steele and Tony Toya. Deb loved visiting her grandparents and was always eager to help them.

They had both worked on railroads in New Mexico and Arizona, and later in life they farmed. They taught Deb the importance of hard work. One of Deb's favorite memories is spending time with her grandfather in his fields. He grew corn and raised fruit trees, including peach and apple trees. Growing food in the Southwest is challenging because of low rainfall. Pulling weeds and knowing when to water crops is key. Haaland remembers, "It was in the cornfields with my grandfather where I learned the importance of water and protecting our resources and where I gained a deep respect for the Earth."

Pueblo Foundations

There is a common Pueblo belief about corn, also known as maize. Without corn there are no people to sing and dance. Without people to sing and dance there is no rain. Without rain there is no corn. This relationship captures the interdependence of plants and people. For centuries, people across the Americas grew and traded with corn, seeds, and other plants. Corn is a particularly valued food because it can be eaten as is, ground to make bread, or stored for the winter months to make stews. For Pueblo people, these agricultural practices remain strong and are deeply tied to community values. Villages regularly hold corn dances. Dances honor life and give life. Corn is viewed as the mother who provides life to all beings. In many Pueblo languages, the name for the stalk of the corn is the same name for a human's body and arms.

Like many Indigenous people, her grandparents had attended boarding schools run by the US government. For many decades, the US government had tried to force Native American children to leave their traditions behind and blend into white American culture. Deb heard stories from her grandparents and other community members about their experiences at boarding schools.

Boarding schools often removed children from their families, cut them off from their heritage, and forced them to speak English. Despite this, Deb's grandparents continued practicing K'awaika beliefs and traditions. Their K'awaika identity could not be erased. Deb's grandparents shared the K'awaika values of perseverance and determination, which laid the groundwork for her future.

Another of Deb's favorite childhood activities was participating in Pueblo customs and ceremonies at Mesita, one of the small K'awaika villages. Many community gatherings focused on good health, not only for K'awaika people but for all people and all living things.

Deb loved being outside. She hiked on the mesas and climbed rocks. Each time her family moved, she explored and learned about a new place. Being outdoors shaped her perspective. As she grew up, she recognized the importance of spending time outdoors with family and community, and she understood the need to be a steward of the land. Taking care of the land made it possible for people to grow food, use other important resources, and build strong communities over many generations.

FINDING HER PASSION

Deb attended thirteen public schools before graduating from high school in Albuquerque. At graduation, Haaland wasn't sure what she wanted to do. She worked at service jobs, but it was hard to make enough money to pay her bills. So Haaland decided to go to college. Then she would have more job opportunities.

Neither of her parents had attended college, so she didn't have much help with the application process. But she was determined. Haaland was accepted to the University of New Mexico. Even though her classes were challenging, she enjoyed learning. Her hard work paid off, and she became the first person in her family to graduate from college. She earned a degree in English in 1994.

Haaland earned two degrees from the University of New Mexico.

Four days after graduating, Haaland gave birth to her daughter, Somáh. Being a single mom was challenging, but Haaland was determined to provide for her daughter. When Somáh was two, Haaland started a small business selling homemade salsa. She named it Pueblo Salsa. She brought her daughter along as she drove around the state selling her product. It was important for Haaland to have flexible work hours so that she could also care for Somáh. Sometimes she didn't make as much money as she needed, so she received some help from government programs.

Haaland also took an interest in politics. In 2002 she closely followed the US Senate elections. In South Dakota,

Haaland made and canned her own salsa for her business.

Lakota voters supported Senator Tim Johnson, and he won reelection by just 528 votes. Each Lakota voter had made a difference in the close race. Haaland remembered, "When I saw what the Indian vote had done in South Dakota, I said, I bet we can do that here."

She decided it was time to continue her education. She enrolled in law school at the University of New Mexico and graduated in 2006. In law school, she focused on Native American law—the legal relationships between the United States and Native American nations. Her passion for this area of law and history helped her choose a clear path forward in public service.

WORKING FOR THE PEOPLE

Service is a core value among many Indigenous peoples. They are taught that they have a responsibility to help others and to take care of the environment for future generations. For Haaland, service also meant getting involved in community and advocacy work to help people vote.

She started out as a phone volunteer, working in campaign offices and calling voters. In 2008 she volunteered for Barack Obama's presidential campaign. She worked diligently to get every person she could to register and vote. Obama won the election, and in 2012 Haaland became the Native American vote director for Obama's reelection campaign.

Native American Voting Rights

When New Mexico became a state in 1912, the state constitution said that Native Americans living on reservations could not vote in elections. In 1948 World War II veteran and Isleta Pueblo citizen Miguel Trujillo tried to register to vote but was denied. He thought that was unfair, so he went to court. He won his case, and Native Americans were officially allowed to vote. But many continued to face barriers to voting. Haaland recognized early on in her career that voting can make a powerful difference in communities. In 2017 the New Mexico state legislature created the Native American Voting Task Force to help remove barriers to voting. When Haaland won her US House seat—thanks in part to the task force's efforts— she thanked Trujillo in her victory speech.

In addition to state and federal elections, Haaland continued to be involved with local politics. She was the first chairwoman elected to the Laguna Development Corporation Board of Directors, a K'awaika-owned business created to strengthen the K'awaika community and its economy. As chairwoman, she supervised operations for the second-largest tribal gaming business in New Mexico. She also successfully pushed for environmentally friendly business practices. Haaland served as the tribal administrator for the San Felipe

Haaland meets with a representative of an organization in New Mexico in 2014.

Pueblo from 2013 to 2015. She made sure the day-to-day work of the K'awaika government ran smoothly, and she helped different offices communicate and work together on projects.

Throughout her career in public service, Haaland has broken barriers and opened doors for future generations. In 2014 Haaland accepted an offer to run for lieutenant governor of New Mexico. She teamed up with Gary King, the Democratic Party's candidate for governor. This made her the first Native American on a New Mexico gubernatorial ticket in the state's history. As King and Haaland campaigned, they talked about what they would do if they won the election. Their goals included raising the minimum wage and creating jobs to help families. They didn't win, but the experience was a learning opportunity for Haaland. She knew her work in public service was not done.

Haaland enjoyed working in politics and encouraged others to get involved. She said, "My passion for getting people in underrepresented communities to vote just grew in every single election year." In 2015 she was elected to a two-year term as the chair of the Democratic Party of New Mexico. Under her leadership, Democrats reclaimed control of the New Mexico House of Representatives.

Haaland was also following the news about the Dakota Access Pipeline, a major oil pipeline project. The pipeline company changed the planned route after white people living in Bismarck, North Dakota, raised concerns about oil leaks. If the pipeline leaked, oil could poison the local water supply or damage the surrounding land. The pipeline's new route would be on the northern border of the Standing Rock Indian Reservation. But when Dakota people who lived there voiced concerns, the company ignored them. Many people thought that was a racist decision.

Members of the Standing Rock Sioux Nation still

In 2016 activists hold up signs to protest the new route for the Dakota Access Pipeline.

hoped to stop the pipeline route. They explained that the pipeline's construction would destroy natural resources. They also stated that once the pipeline started operating, it would pose a serious risk to their water supply and to the very survival of the nation.

Standing Rock Sioux leaders started a protest camp where people could gather to oppose the pipeline. Soon Native Americans and other environmental activists from all over the US went there to show their support. Haaland went too. She strongly believed in protecting one of Earth's most valuable resources: water. All people need clean water to live, so this was not just a Standing Rock issue.

A SEAT AT THE TABLE

Haaland wanted to continue to help and serve the people of New Mexico. After finishing her term as the state's Democratic Party chair, Haaland announced she was running for a seat in the US House of Representatives. Haaland started early and worked hard to get her message out. Protecting the environment and slowing climate change were important parts of her campaign. Haaland described herself as a lifelong environmentalist.

On November 6, 2018, Deb Haaland won the election. Another Native American woman, Sharice Davids, who is enrolled with the Ho-Chunk Nation of Wisconsin, also won a congressional seat. Haaland and Davids became the first two Native American women elected to Congress.

During her years in Congress, Haaland worked hard. She served on several committees and subcommittees that focused on specific issues. She was on the House Committee on Natural Resources, which writes laws and policies about energy resources, public lands, Native American affairs, water, wildlife, and resource management. Haaland was a strong advocate for environmental justice. She pushed for the Department of the Interior to report on how its activities impact environmental and health issues.

A Representative's Job

Each member of the US House of Representatives is elected to a two-year term by the people from a specific congressional district in their home state. Representatives write laws and serve on committees. To be elected, a representative must be at least twenty-five years old, a US citizen for at least seven years, and a resident of the state they represent.

Haaland was also passionate about ending violence against Indigenous people, especially women. The murder rate for Native American and Alaska Native women is about ten times higher than the US national average. Indigenous women also experience high rates of domestic violence, and many Indigenous women who go missing are never found. Haaland wanted to bring attention to these issues and give communities more resources to prevent violence.

Haaland supported Savanna's Act, which aims to improve the Department of Justice's response to missing or murdered Native Americans.

Haaland explained, "The stakes are too high to keep the status quo in place." She wanted to create change "by providing resources and information-sharing amendments to keep survivors of domestic violence safe from harm, ultimately preventing future cases." Due to the hard work of Haaland and others, the House of Representatives passed the reauthorization of the Violence Against Women Act (VAWA) in 2019.

In 2020 Haaland was the lead sponsor of the Not Invisible Act, which passed in both houses of Congress. The Not Invisible Act created an advisory committee on violent crime. The committee's job was to work with the US Department of the Interior and Department of Justice. It would recommend better ways to handle murder and missing persons cases involving Indigenous people, and it would suggest ways to prevent violence against Indigenous people.

The people of New Mexico were excited about the progress Haaland was making in Washington. But the COVID-19 pandemic made some people hesitant to get out and vote. As the 2020 election approached, Haaland's campaign encouraged voters to vote early and send in absentee ballots if they couldn't vote in person on Election Day. In November of that year, Haaland won reelection. She said, "We did everything we could do to get voters to the polls. That was our main concern, just making sure that everybody voted and had a way to vote and understood how they could vote." But it wasn't long before her name was being mentioned for a position in President Joe Biden's new administration.

STEWARD OF THE LAND

After Biden was elected president in the 2020 election, he started thinking about his cabinet nominations. The Cabinet of the United States is part of the executive branch. It includes the leaders of the fifteen executive departments, who work closely with the president. The president nominates and Congress confirms each department head, known as a cabinet secretary.

Haaland was serving as the vice chair of the House Committee on Natural Resources. She has always had a close connection to land. Many of her ancestors were farmers, and her parents and grandparents taught her to value and respect the land. She also had experience in working with diverse communities and passing legislation. Biden wanted someone with these skills and values to be his secretary of the interior, and he nominated Haaland for the role.

The Department of the Interior

The Department of the Interior (DOI) was established in 1849. It combined several existing offices, including the General Land Office and the Bureau of Indian Affairs. Later, the DOI's duties grew to include overseeing the census, management of territorial governments, colonizing western lands, and more. In the twenty-first century, the DOI manages federal lands and resources. The person in charge of the DOI is called the secretary of the interior and is a member of the Cabinet of the United States.

Many Native Americans were excited about Haaland's nomination. They sent tens of thousands of letters expressing their support of Haaland. Social media users started the hashtag #DebForInterior. Others created artwork. Some even projected her image onto the Main Interior Building with the words, "The Future We Need."

On February 23-24, 2021, the Senate held hearings to learn more about Haaland. At the hearings, she began by acknowledging that the Senate was meeting on the ancestral homelands of the Nacotchtank, Anacostan, and Piscataway people. She promised to be a leader with integrity and to work with people of all backgrounds. She said, "I will honor the sovereignty of tribal nations and recognize their part in America's story, and I'll be a fierce

Haaland speaks during her Senate confirmation hearings in 2021.

advocate for our public lands. I believe we all have a stake in the future of our country, and I believe that every one of us—Republicans, Democrats, and Independents—shares a common bond: our love for the outdoors and a desire and obligation to keep our nation livable for future generations."

On March 15, 2021, the Senate confirmed Haaland as the secretary of the interior by a vote of 51-40. She got right to work.

Biden asked Haaland to research the boundaries of two national monuments, Bears Ears and Grand Staircase-Escalante. National monuments are unique and important lands that a US president decides to protect.

The Grosvenor Arch at the Grand Staircase-Escalante National Monument

Rock art at Bears Ears National Monument

President Bill Clinton created Grand Staircase-Escalante in 1996. President Obama created Bears Ears National Monument in 2016. In 2017 President Donald Trump reduced the size of Bears Ears by 85 percent and the size of Grand Staircase-Escalante by about 50 percent. This allowed energy companies to mine more uranium and increase drilling for oil and gas.

Haaland decided to visit these lands herself. In April 2021, she went to both monuments. She met with tribal and state leaders to discuss the importance of these places. Bears Ears has special meaning for several Native American nations. The area has extraordinary rock art, historic cliff dwellings, and important cultural resources.

Both Grand Staircase-Escalante and Bears Ears have unique varieties of plant and animal life, including rare hanging gardens.

After her visit, Haaland wrote a report recommending that Biden return the monuments to their previous sizes. She said, "It's our obligation to make sure that we protect lands for future generations so they can have the same experiences that the governor and I experienced today. This place is filled with cultural heritage. That cultural heritage belongs to every single American." Biden agreed with Haaland. He restored the earlier boundaries of Bears Ears and Grand Staircase-Escalante monuments. Future generations will continue to enjoy visiting these special places.

On November 19, 2021, Haaland formally declared *squaw* to be a derogatory term. The word *squaw* originally came from a word for "woman" from the Algonquian language. But it has been long used as a sexist and offensive term for Native American women. Haaland knew that many federal lands have this word in their names and that it is painful for many Native Americans to visit those places. She ordered a task force to choose new names for valleys, lakes, creeks, and other sites on federal lands that use the word. She believes it is important to remove hurtful words from place-names because these lands should be places where everyone can enjoy and celebrate the outdoors. More than 650 federal sites will need new names, so this project will take a long time to complete.

New Names

Deb Haaland's idea to change place-names with offensive language is not new. Some places have already undergone name changes. For example, in 2008 the name of a mountain in Arizona was changed from Squaw Peak to Piestewa Peak. The new name honors Lori Piestewa, a member of the Hopi Nation. She was a US Army soldier who was killed in action in Iraq in 2003. She was the first Native American woman to die in combat while serving in the US military.

WORKING FOR CHANGE

The issue of violence against Indigenous women continued to weigh on Haaland. She was proud of the work she had done in Congress but knew she needed to do more. She wanted justice for murdered and missing Indigenous women, and she wanted to prevent future abuse, murders, and disappearances. On April 1, 2021, she announced the formation of the Missing and Murdered Unit (MMU) within the Bureau of Indian Affairs Office of Justice Services. The MMU would help coordinate the complex network of agencies involved in solving and prosecuting cases of missing and murdered Native Americans and Alaska Natives. The unit would put more resources into investigating these cases.

"Violence against Indigenous peoples is a crisis that has been underfunded for decades," said Haaland. "Far too often, murders and missing persons cases in Indian country go unsolved and unaddressed, leaving families and communities devastated." She added, "The new MMU unit will provide the resources and leadership to prioritize these cases and

In 2021 Haaland discusses ways to reduce violence against Native American women.

coordinate resources to hold people accountable, keep our communities safe, and provide closure for families."

Haaland had never forgotten her grandparents' stories about US federal boarding schools for Indigenous children. She felt it was important for everyone to know the history of these schools. On June 22, 2021, Haaland announced the Federal Boarding School Initiative, which would research the boarding schools and write reports for the public.

Beginning with the Civilization Fund Act of 1819 and continuing through at least the 1960s, the United States created and paid for boarding schools for Native Americans. The number of children who attended these schools is unknown. Sometimes parents gave permission for their children to attend these schools. But often they did not, and US authorities forced the children to go anyway.

The schools had different rules over time, but the main goal of these schools was to culturally assimilate Native American children. This meant separating children from their families and making them ashamed about their identity. Students were often punished harshly for speaking their native languages. Many students were physically or sexually abused by people who worked at the schools.

An unknown number of children died at these schools. And in many cases, their families weren't told what had happened or where their children were buried. These unanswered questions haunted Indigenous families and communities. Even for children who eventually returned home, the trauma of boarding school could have a lifelong impact.

In many Native American families, multiple generations of children have attended boarding schools. This is the case for Haaland's family. Her great-grandfather was taken to Carlisle Indian Industrial School, a boarding school in Pennsylvania. Her mother's parents were taken away from their families without permission and sent to boarding school when they were only eight years old. They were not allowed to return for five long years. Her grandfather became a railroad mechanic in Arizona, but he continued to practice Pueblo ceremonies and traditions. As a college student, Haaland talked with her grandmother in detail about her experiences at boarding school. It was emotional for both of them. Haaland realized that everyone should

Resisting Assimilation

The very first US-government-run boarding school for Native American children was Carlisle Indian Industrial School in Carlisle, Pennsylvania. It opened in 1879. Civil War veteran Richard Henry Pratt was the superintendent. His motto was "kill the Indian, and save the man." This meant complete cultural assimilation. Students had to convert to Christianity, wear Western clothes, and speak English. They also experienced harsh physical discipline and solitary confinement. Partly in response to this treatment, a number of graduates became activists for Native American rights. For example, Lakota author and educator Luther Standing Bear argued that Lakota traditions were valuable and should continue to be practiced. He criticized many US government laws and policies, including those that outlawed Native American religions. He said that the history and culture of Native Americans should be included in public schools. His writings and lectures increased public awareness and created popular support for changing US government policies.

know about the history of these schools and about the effect they still have on Indigenous families and communities.

Haaland acknowledged that learning about this history is hard but necessary. "I launched the Federal Indian Boarding School Initiative to begin the long healing process that our country must address in order to build a future we can all be proud to embrace," said Haaland.

One goal of the Federal Boarding School Initiative is to find out as much as possible about the children who died at the schools so that their families can finally know what happened and where they are buried. The research will also investigate the lasting impacts of these schools. One impact, for instance, has been a big decrease in the

In 2021 Haaland speaks at a ceremony to honor the Native American children who died at the Carlisle Indian Industrial School.

number of Native Americans who can speak their native languages. The first report was scheduled to be finished in 2022.

LOOKING AHEAD

Haaland continues to remember and honor her Pueblo core values, which center on family and land stewardship. On August 28, 2021, she married her longtime partner, Skip Sayre, surrounded by family and friends at the Hyatt Tamaya Regency Resort & Spa on the Santa Ana Pueblo. Her early experiences of being outdoors and recognizing

Haaland waves to the crowd after participating in a totem pole blessing ceremony in 2021.

the beauty of nature have stuck with her. She recalls, "The best memories I have are of me and my grandpa, picking worms off ears of corn in the field below our village. In front of us, a towering red mesa and a sky that won't quit. We're eating the sweetest peaches in the shade of a tree."

Running for a Reason

Haaland began running for exercise in about 2000, but running is not just a hobby for her. She is practicing a Pueblo tradition. Historically, Pueblo runners ran from house to house and to different communities to share important news. In modern times, Pueblo villages hold foot races. Haaland enjoys running in many different places, including the Anacostia River Trail near her home in Washington, DC, and the Bosque Trail in Albuquerque. In 2021 she ran in the Boston Marathon, which was held on October 11, Indigenous Peoples' Day. The route was on ancestral homelands of the Massachusett, Mashpee Wampanoag, and Pawtucket Nations. Haaland thought this race was special. She wrote, "I will run for missing and murdered Indigenous peoples and their families, the victims of the Indian boarding schools, and the promise that our voices are being heard and will have a part in an equitable and just future in this new era."

Haaland entered public service to make a difference in people's lives. Her community organizing and professional training were inspired by what her parents and grandparents taught her. Reflecting on her success, Haaland stated, "As a kid, I never would have imagined today. I will leave the ladder down behind me so girls of color know they can be anything they want to be."

Haaland is determined to include as many people as possible in local and national politics. Haaland wants to inspire people of all backgrounds and ages to get involved in issues like climate protection that impact all communities. She will continue working hard to make communities safer for everyone, to honor the complex history of the United States and Indigenous nations, and to protect the land for future generations.

Haaland continues to speak out for Indigenous rights.

IMPORTANT DATES

1960 Debra Anne Haaland is born to Mary Toya and John David "Dutch" Haaland on December 2.

1994 Haaland graduates from the University of New Mexico with a degree in English. The same year, Haaland gives birth to a daughter, Somáh Haaland.

2006 Haaland earns a law degree from the University of New Mexico School of Law.

2012 Haaland works as New Mexico's vote director for Native Americans for President Barack Obama's reelection campaign.

2014 Haaland runs for lieutenant governor of New Mexico on the Democratic ticket but is defeated by the Republican ticket.

2015 Haaland is elected to a two-year term as the chair of the Democratic Party of New Mexico.

2016 Haaland goes to the Standing Rock Indian Reservation to meet with local Dakota leaders and joins the opposition to the Dakota Access Pipeline.

2019 Haaland is sworn into the US House of Representatives, representing the First Congressional District of New Mexico.

2021 Haaland is nominated, confirmed, and sworn in as the US secretary of the interior. She starts the Missing and Murdered Unit and announces the Federal Boarding School Initiative. The same year, Haaland marries her longtime partner, Skip Sayre.

SOURCE NOTES

9   Scott Stump, "Rep. Debra Haaland Wore Indigenous Dress at Historic Swearing-In Ceremony as Interior Secretary," *Today*, March 19, 2021, https://www.today.com/style/rep-debra-haaland -wore-indigenous-dress-she made-cabinet-history-t212251.

10 Yvette Cabrera, "Deb Haaland Is Making Room for Marginalized Communities in the Interior Department," Grist, April 19, 2021, https://grist.org/equity/deb-haaland-environmental-justice-interior -department-new-mexico/.

15 Deb Haaland, "Statement of Debra Anne Haaland, Nominee for the Position of Secretary of the Department of the Interior, before the Committee on Energy and Natural Resources, United States Senate," Senate Committee on Energy and Natural Resources, February 23, 2021, https://www.energy.senate.gov /services/files/D80C6AC0-D4F4-4E7E-9D1D-C7DD06E93411.

19 Jenni Monet, "Deb Haaland, a Living Testament," *Sierra*, September 15, 2021, https://www.sierraclub.org/sierra/2021-4 -fall/feature/deb-haaland-living-testament.

21 Colleen Heild, "Haaland Says She Shares Struggles of Many in NM," *Albuquerque Journal*, October 1, 2018, https://www .abqjournal.com/1227787/haaland-says-she-shares-struggles-of -many-in-nm.html.

25 "Malinda Williams, "Honor Missing and Murdered Indigenous Women," *Taos News*, September 4, 2019, https://www.taosnews .com/opinion/columns/honor-missing-and-murdered-indigenous -women/article_eb2de709-ab69-5166-b3a5-ea9c965d248b.html.

26 Kendra Chamberlain, "Deb Haaland Easily Wins Reelection to U.S. House of Representatives," NM Political Report, November 3, 2020, https://nmpoliticalreport.com/2020/11/03/deb-haaland-easily-wins-reelection-to-u-s-house-of-representatives/.

28–29 "Watch Deb Haaland's Full Opening Statement at Confirmation Hearing for Interior Secretary," *Washington Post*, February 23, 2021, https://www.washingtonpost.com/video/politics/watch-deb-haalands-full-opening-statement-at-confirmation-hearing-for-interior-secretary/2021/02/23/70289a21-2249-4aaf-8f43-0b7146cf374f_video.html.

31 Joshua Partlow, "Tourists and Looters Descend on Bears Ears as Biden Mulls Protections: Interior Secretary Haaland Visits Utah Monument amid Controversy over Whether to Restore Boundaries Shrunk by Trump," *Washington Post*, April 8, 2021, https://www.washingtonpost.com/nation/2021/04/08/bears-ears-haaland/.

33 "Secretary Haaland Creates New Missing & Murdered Unit to Pursue Justice for Missing or Murdered American Indians and Alaska Natives," US Department of the Interior, April 1, 2021, https://www.doi.gov/news/secretary-haaland-creates-new-missing-murdered-unit-pursue-justice-missing-or-murdered-american.

35 Deb Haaland, "Opinion: Deb Haaland; My Grandparents Were Stolen from Their Families as Children. We Must Learn about This History.," *Washington Post*, June 11, 2021, https://www.washingtonpost.com/opinions/2021/06/11/deb-haaland-indigenous-boarding-schools/.

36 US Department of the Interior, "Interior Department to Hold Tribal Consultations on the Federal Boarding School Initiative, U.S. Department of Interior," news release, September 30, 2021, https://www.doi.gov/pressreleases/interior-department-hold-tribal-consultations-federal-boarding-school-initiative.

38 Deb Haaland, "Who Speaks for You?" YouTube video, 7:49, posted by TEDx Talks, December 22, 2016, https://www.youtube.com/watch?v=KkEY6zaqdlM&t=210s.

38 Diane Bird, "Leaving the Ladder Down," *El Palacio*, Winter 2019, https://www.elpalacio.org/2020/01/leaving-the-ladder-down/.

39 Deb Haaland, "Opinion: Running the Boston Marathon to Remember Indigenous Peoples' Day," *Boston Globe*, October 10, 2021, https://www.bostonglobe.com/2021/10/10/opinion/running-boston-marathon-remember-indigenous-peoples-day/.

SELECTED BIBLIOGRAPHY

Benallie, Kalle. "US Boarding Schools to Be Investigated." *Indian Country Today*, June 22, 2021. https://indiancountrytoday.com/news/us-boarding-schools-to-be-investigated.

Bryan, Susan Montoya. "Deb Haaland Seeks to Rid US of Derogatory Place Names." *Indian Country Today,* November 19, 2021. https://indiancountrytoday.com/news/deb-haaland-seeks-to-rid-us-of-derogatory-place-names.

Cabral, Sam. "Deb Haaland: America's First Native Cabinet Secretary." BBC, March 16, 2021. https://www.bbc.com/news/world-us-canada-56421097.

"Deb Haaland: One for the History Books." *Mirage Magazine,* November 3, 2021. https://mirage.unm.edu/deb-haaland-one-for-the-history-books/.

Duoos, Kayla. "The Ribbon Skirt: Part 1." Leech Lake News, September 30, 2019. https://www.leechlakenews.com/2019/09/30/the-ribbon-skirt-part-1/.

Haaland, Deb. "Opinion: Deb Haaland; My Grandparents Were Stolen from Their Families as Children. We Must Learn about This History." *Washington Post,* June 11, 2021. https://www.washingtonpost.com/opinions/2021/06/11/deb-haaland-indigenous-boarding-schools/.

——"Tribal Justice: Honoring Indigenous Dispute Resolution (Symposium Keynote Address)." *Tribal Law Journal* 20, no. 1 (2020). https://digitalrepository.unm.edu/tlj/vol20/iss1/2.

Jones, Rachel. "Inside Deb Haaland's Historic Bid to Become One of the First Native Congresswomen." *National Geographic*, November 7, 2018. https://www.nationalgeographic.com/culture/article/debra-haaland-first-native-american-congresswoman-new-mexico-midterm-election.

Stump, Scott. "Rep. Debra Haaland Wore Indigenous Dress at Historic Swearing-In Ceremony as Interior Secretary." *Today,* March 19, 2021. https://www.today.com/style/rep-debra-haaland-wore-indigenous-dress-she-made-cabinet-history-t212251.

LEARN MORE

Anderson, Jennifer Joline. *Exploring Voting and Elections*. Minneapolis: Lerner Publications, 2020.

Britannica Kids: Deb Haaland
https://kids.britannica.com/students/article/Deb-Haaland/633204

Dunbar-Ortiz, Roxanne. *An Indigenous Peoples' History of the United States for Young People*. Adapted by Jean Mendoza and Debbie Reese. Boston: Beacon, 2019.

Indian Pueblo Cultural Center
https://indianpueblo.org

Keene, Adrienne. *Notable Native People: 50 Indigenous Leaders, Dreamers, and Changemakers from Past and Present*. Emeryville, CA: Ten Speed, 2021.

Kiddle: Deb Haaland
https://kids.kiddle.co/Deb_Haaland

Treuer, Anton. *Everything You Wanted to Know about Indians but Were Afraid to Ask: Young Readers Edition*. Montclair, NJ: Levine Querido, 2021.

INDEX